The Angel's Lament

The Angel's Lament

Poems of Chonggi Mah

Translated by Youngshil Cho

Homa & Sekey Books
Paramus, New Jersey

FIRST EDITION

Copyright © 2020 by Chonggi Mah
Originally published in 2020 (천사의 탄식) by Moonji Publishing Co., Ltd.
English translation copyright © 2024 by Cho Young-Shil

This book is published with the support of the Literature Translation Institute of Korea (LTI Korea).

The cover art is a detail of an angel from the *Baronci Altarpiece* by Raphael.

Library of Congress Cataloging-in-Publication Data

Names: Ma, Chong-gi, 1939- author.
Title: The angel's lament / poems of Chonggi Mah.
Other titles: Ch'ŏnsa ŭi t'ansik. English
Description: First edition. | Paramus, New Jersey : Homa & Sekey Books, 2024.
Identifiers: LCCN 2023058688 | ISBN 9781622461189 (paperback)
Subjects: LCGFT: Poetry.
Classification: LCC PL992.49.C4 C38 2024 | DDC 895.71/4--dc23/eng/20240228
LC record available at https://lccn.loc.gov/2023058688

Published by Homa & Sekey Books
3rd Floor, North Tower
Mack-Cali Center III
140 E. Ridgewood Ave.
Paramus, NJ 07652

Tel: 201-261-8810, 800-870-HOMA
Fax: 201-261-8890
Email: info@homabooks.com
Website: www.homabooks.com

Printed in the USA
1 3 5 7 9 10 8 6 4 2

Author's Note

I have collected the poems I have written and published since my last poetry book, the weary words and writings living beyond mountains, across seas, and now I send them to my home country. It took me five years, but since that is my average speed, I would like to believe I have not been sluggish. My thanks go to you who will read these poems.

Chonggi Mah
September, 2020

Author's Note

Contents

PART III

PART I

Honor of Dew

Dew is honor of my flesh,
comes early in darkness
and leaves before morning comes into full bloom.
Having lived abroad invisible,
with the day breaking I take off my torn armor.
Dead dew is a few drops of water,
what a difficult and fearful resolution
to love in all earnest.

I came to a foreign country on borrowed money.
Worked day and night, paid back the loan,
sold out remnant lonely springtime of my youth
resenting the country to which I wouldn't be able to return.
The one-way road I've taken is but a solitary way lived
without pretext or remorse or dismay or flattery,
and the dew that neither fled nor hid itself but vanished.
Where is it gone, before I search
a rainbow of dew comes into bloom.
Like a medal, like the eye of a prophet
standing unflinching where all have left!

Lenten Butterfly

I didn't know why the butterfly breathes not a word.
Nor knew that it can't fly for the body weight
if the torrent of words be glued to the wings.
A butterfly can't live forever like a green caterpillar.
A few smiles, sound muffled, so as to enter into a flower,
and a mute mouth unanswered, there blossoms spring.

A butterfly bowing in consolation of death of magnolia's
    daughter.
I should have wound it up in prayer while climbing a rocky
    mountain?
The silence in which I climbed the mountain, sweating
    blood,
rather shielded me, comforted me. Gazing up,
Love endures, so saying, all the while in pains of obedience
whole body is torn apart, breaks down over and over.

Sunlight, Lent around the corner, butterfly unfurling
    wings,
thy breath known to forgive all trespasses
surely sets my wings' bearings right.
Falling, rising, then falling again,
all deaths coming to an end; vernal noonday.

A Night Walk in Sinseol-dong

Late night as I walked to the bar agreed on,
it was so dark along the rivulet in Sinseol-dong
with no street light, my companion said he was scared
but how very happy and restful I was.

The medical science I learned all I wanted was not a learn-
    ing
but a hard stealing into human groaning,
sinking into that darkness.
A long road of sinking, then getting soaked.

Soaked age, long waiting,
but the days unscathed shall come together
as flower or fruit, to engrave the name;
I have no remorse even if this night walking mark my end.

The wounds in my foot-sole rough and parched
are carapaces of self-reproach swept by floods of people,
though I walk on guided by the feet of a traveler fallen ill
the brook murmuring follows no more.

Today the eyes of good night shine,
to whom even the cold greets at ease.
That light must be our bar
where restful words and faces mingle together into one.

Loving with all sincerity you have
is shunned by all, saying *That's extreme stupidity*;
the night walking in Sinseol-dong sinking deep in me,
who left the flawless city to come here.

Leave-taking of the Seas

The sea leaving the shore
cries and cries under its breath
deep into the night, rueful to leave,
but I figure it does not yet sense
that when it grows up in some years
it shall return as tide.

Oh the sea therefore crying sadly,
anyhow we live not knowing where we're going,
not even a moment's course.
I can only assure myself of and believe
the journey expecting
that I will meet you.

Oh the sea wishing to return, pawing the shore,
then leaving blooded,
so is all our appearance;
the bone-weary sea's wet eyes
are gazing at the naked body of days past.
I lift up my body that has tumbled down
and stand before the sea that will return.

Time in Prison

After taking some four month's long journey I return
    home,
open the door that's been fast locked and enter an empty
    room;
the airs collected roomful, wilting along the way,
raise a hubbub, saying How in the world could you lock
    us up so,
hard to breathe, we thought we're dying.
(What if I open the door after a year.)
While at it, I opened the curtain, opened the window wide;
by ones and twos, airs in deep coma begin to stir up,
and now bulked up, bounce about and even sing.

Forbear confining long whatever, whoever,
in my youth I too lived in prison, gnashing my teeth.
Dim air, gloomy walls, and fury hard to breathe,
may no country forcibly imprison, threaten, and oppress
air or reed that live guiltless.
Forbear overthrowing the other's unguarded life
by however big a name or idea or power.
Forbear confining, or striking
even if you suddenly find living hard and painful.
Though they say the lost future days wax cold miles away,
still, still!

Gallipoli 1

A green hill looking down the Aegean coast far away, graves of some twenty New Zealand soldiers buried in a sunny side of south of Turkey are dozing off over one hundred years, bashful of their discolored tombstones. Quiet noontime with no passenger, aged tombstones at times open their eyes awake, look around. *Where is it here? In what direction is my country I left?* Families behind, they sailed over weeks, engaged in bloody fight for their side, against the enemy side. Why did they have to fight, killing each other? The query of the fighters landed dead in Gallipoli each year broke open in scentless dandelions.

Naturally, Turkey that received their bodies into the ground, and their homeland also seem oblivious of them all; dandelions, profusely abloom this year again, allay dusty nostalgia. What marks could the fighters leave behind, buried on the hillside of Izmir far beyond Gallipoli hellish with 500 thousands slayed. With no excuse, they died knifed and shot and bombed and drowned. The next day I went to the graveside again, ran my hand over a small tombstone barely showing the name, and my palm was full of its tears. The gravestone leaning into me whispers to me. What it says is wet, and so feeble.

There were a good many sheep in the ranch where I grew up. My mother and my wife and heaven and earth knew nothing but sheepherding. My country bid me go and I left home, not knowing where I was going; got all bloody in hell. Only after death, I came to grasp war is bad. It was war that really should have died. Beware of the one holding that he alone is in the right. Beware of the real intent of the one crying for ideals or justice only. That long war ended, a

6

hundred years have passed, but my body still hurts. I miss my mother and my wife, unfair for me. A patch of sunflowers yonder, too, shun the sun in broad daylight, their heads bowed low.

Gallipoli 2

Out of despair and doubts over the brutal six months' Battle of Gallipoli while reading a book on World War 1, I eventually went in person along the Aegean coast into the land of Turkey, roamed about a good while. It was upsetting to suddenly see a scatter of dilapidated graves of the many soldiers from Australia, New Zealand—distant countries—who died and now lie buried over one hundred years; then I remembered that one of those days I stayed around there was my blood grandfather's Memorial Day. When did I last visit his graveyard, I realize it was nearly 70 years ago.

The memory how I in my second year in elementary school joined my father visiting our ancestral burial ground, cutting grass, and bowing before my blood grandparents and great-grandfather. People now call that place the demilitarized zone, or DMZ, and I reckon my great-grandparents haven't seen their offspring bowing before them ever since, just waiting and waiting under the tangle of various nameless wild animals and untended brushes. By now they may have given up the hope of seeing us. As we, even if unification occur wouldn't be able to find the location of their graves after all.

The Turkish coast where bare sea seems vaster, I turned eastward and bowed low toward my grandfather twice, halfway once, offered a glass of liquor which was but Turkish beer, then spent several days brooding over the many graves forsaken in improper places. By the way, recent news detailed that, possibly because of Aegean fishes reportedly wiped out, 300 refugees from Syria, Afghanistan and Africa, wandering in dug-out canoes just this month, and over three thousand last year drowned in the Aegean Sea to death.

So soon I've reached the twilight age. I see people die anywhere. Things seen clearly keep paling, and what does that blood-red afterglow have to tell me who has lived running around all my life. Not all people can die in the countries of their birth. Only the ones selected and lucky sleep warm. Granted that heaven allow any plot in any country, if not a heaven-sent spot, I guess we no longer need to sway with every wind. And there will be a day when I, dancing tum-tumming, will meet my great-grandparents also, whom I've neglected for apparent busyness.

Spring in That House

I realize there in that house in the alley I frequent
lived a flower tree.
Perhaps an empty space, with shades gone,
one, then another, flowers that have bloomed are so
    bright
I can very well tell just by the sight of one blossom
the name of the tree whose trunk I cannot see.

Is that flower a boundless world,
spring that has ended a long wandering and returned
achingly captivates me again;
the sunlight that has lived in hiding comes near
to caress earth with warm hand.
Words kept unsaid in my breast
slowly begin to spread out in all directions.

Now it'll be all right.
All preparations are completed.
Spring begins to perch on clouds,
old promises brush off dust
to awake my life as I return home;
wintry dusk, as if grudging,
abandons its plot and leaves the place.

Stranger's House

For sure a wind blew at first.
No particular direction or place,
I heard whirlwind all over.
Tree-branches shook and broke off,
leaves of motley colors blew about.
Soon lightning flashed from all sides,
thunderclap shook the age with despair
holding it must go its own way anyway.

The peal of thunder seemed to die away, then
in the end torrential rain fell.
In the rain I couldn't see front or back, up or down,
so it wildly beset me, a youth with no home.
When the rain filling up heaven and earth softly stopped
night without a word came between us.
We lay together under a quilt of darkness
in which we could see neither past nor future nor today.
Was that fear, or rather uncertainty?
We then very likely tired out, slipped into sleep.
How we so slept endless, dreamless for scores of years.
Waking up, we were old folks bent with age.

I haven't gotten it wrong, have I?
Is it merely something like fate or star
that I run along the edge, soaked; in the beginning,
how severely the wind blew.
Besides the smell stuck at that time
nothing else is left in this house.

Earth from Seoul

1

After 50 years I entered the old home I used to live in as
    a child
and round the teary place saw no one I knew of;
sad in my empty heart, I raked a handful of earth in the
    small yard,
rushed to pocket it, got out of the house.
A handful of my old family's fond voices and laughter,
how soothing and heartwarming it felt.
To nobody I have told that
but insinuated so to my wife
as something might go wrong in my negligence.
Should I happen to go suddenly in an alien land
please ensure to put this handful of earth in my hand.

These days I often sniff the earth in a small box,
sometimes gingerly touch it,
but somehow the beloved earth feels diminishing with
    time;
does it evaporate away from home, or fly off in the wind,
inside I grow anxious with diminishing earth.
Won't it be too meagre to hold in my hand when I leave.
Sometimes it even shines with luster as if saying some-
    thing.
I suppose the hardest thing of all is parting
but when I peer into my earth even parting is tender.
On the road I pass by I see someone too, who left my side.

2

Earth, whether from Seoul or abroad,
is known as the stuff filling human body
even so, does it slowly vanish away
once severed from the earth it has lived with;
why is it so difficult to live alone;
fresh smell flags, then fades,
sinewy muscles that grew flowers are nowhere to be seen.

I do not know how human bonds come to be
but one that is willfully enforced
does not endure.
Perhaps somebody will tell me someday
why earth breaks down, longing for earth.

Chile Raining

On my arrival it rained everyday.
Rainy spells setting in, the city was so enervated
roads and hotels and bakeries and bicycles
and even leisurely coast were being washed out.
I turned into a narrow alley, and lo, an unexpected flower
    garden,
sodden at ease was scent of flowers
come together to live in a parcel with no fixed address.
Flowers having their eyes shut as if trying to sleep,
sound of rain at once sounded like a voice of prayer.
Ah, the report that somebody has overcome this world,
calling me from what a faraway country.
Immersed in Holy Spirit that moves us to tremble head-
    foremost
I entered an antiquated catholic church to shake off cold
    rain.

Taming Gossip 20

Autumn foliage of different colors is said to be due to the sugar component in the tree: much sugar in it tints the foliage nicely; little, poorly; scarce, not at all. So they say the sugar collected in the leaf tints it into beautiful colors, red and yellow and brown. Summer's green leaves with chlorophyl draw in the sun to raise the tree and leaves, and in autumn the tree feeling the chill and short daytime begins to put stashed sugar on leaves. This sugar is thought to color leaves into autumn shades, then to help in their slow falling.

For all that, I suppose evergreen trees which, for want of sugar, disdain the world and don't change their arrogant attitude, are stripped of sweetness or warmth. Probably they don't even know what they lack. Probably the trees cold-bloodied for want of sugar cannot produce fair hue, staying all too cold and cruel even when one holds the trunk wholeheartedly. How fortunate that I don't have such a thing by my side. A tree that shares the warmth at any spare time and gives smile through tacit gestures. A thoughtful look arranging in time a gathering for one's own child. In autumn I have a greater tender feeling for trees whose leaves turn color.

A poem unshapely and deplorable
which I devotedly managed to finish exhausted.
With a trace of warmth still in my heart
I put my arms around it, prizing, caring.
On hearing that I love it, the poem
radiates brightness on the face. Ah,

a word and bodily warmth too is solace.
The tree's finger gives me a jog.

History of Gooseflesh

As I listen to a choral harmony gooseflesh rises
and I rub my aged skin quietly.
From both cheeks down to twin arms
it leaves acute marks, making my hair stand on end.

Oh my skin untrained yet,
what a pity you don't know music and fear are two differ-
    ent things
since gooseflesh is the sign of terror!
Or rather, what a crazy dumb move
attempting to shut the door, feeling only a chill
in an elegant aria in an opera!

Yet once in a while I am thankful.
That my late mother came last night
and silently touched my cheeks.
Gladness overflowing, each thread
of delicate gooseflesh I felt living with me to this day.
When I woke up my senses were still vibrant.

Sure, it's all fine even if you digress sometimes.
It will not injure this smooth town.
Perilous though the age my gooseflesh has lived through
but please keep the world's skin warm always,
misjudge it is soft and good and fair.
See and hear the nuclear explosion raging for war
as something like the *Moonlight* in *Rusalka*.

Oh my skin unevolved
translating emotion as fear
while I listen to music this dusky hour,
feeling cold and fear are identical, about when

do you think 1 will learn history's great reason
that there is something radiant and shining besides fear
that simple things sometimes are the most beautiful things.
And feel the earnestness and beauty of confusion.

A Fugue for a Friend

I wonder if that was really a road;
gasping, sweating,
watching all around with head bowed,
I say I did not even take note of the long days
I've actually lived through. Was it a road.

Pushing forward and casting light, the steps
felt cold; wind blew;
we were heat-weary
but floral scent, rain sounds, light on a river, too,
strewn round the days and nights that are gone by,
I say all that was the deep flesh of one life.

Like jewels we walked long
and temptation, a flower blossoming but in a silent field
and shedding clothes,
a long smile when leaving this world,
that walkway representing the breath
of my friend who died a few days ago.

Vespers

Happier are you,
who merely have a single flower
than a rich man who has many flowers.

Having just one flower
you know the beginning and the end of the flower,
and about when the flower
takes on a hue, about when in secret
it makes fragrance

why it gives a smile when approached,
about what hour it falls asleep,
that enchantment being able to hear
each and all of its breath in sleep,
I say the one who has but only one flower
fully knows the meaning of possession.

Yet when we sometime grow old,
hoary and wizened,
then drop off into twilight shadows,
in whose memory will the exquisite hues and scents
in lifetime remain to live on.
Who will come near
to wake us from our sleep.

Last Day of Winter

Nobody came to visit.
Spring went away and summer passed by.
Growing with their kind, fluttering about
with their kind, they found their companions
to bear diverse fruits.

Afterwards a knocking on the door
was often heard. One moment audible, the next inaudible,
fallen leaves were swept by wind.
Forsaken bonds said to be of no use altogether.
One day, from the evening my surroundings shrank,
and maybe a rhythmic humming, maybe someone coming,
a whispering was heard through the night.
I opened the door to see snow falling.
Wind was busy mixing the night and the snow.

Everything in sight was dreary, but to confess,
that was precisely my entire tough life.
But I was glad it ended up with the white.
Who knows if the patience on my body cells is but a
    weight,
it became difficult for me to take a step, then another.
Gone are the days when I wandered not knowing how to
    endure.

Winter came like that.
Nobody came to visit.
It may be cold remorse piled into snow,
winter night wreathing round my bare body is rather ten-
    der.
Over there the last of winter is drawing near

but whose great kindness are the days to come,
they say one still hears a while after the last breath.
Hard questions raised ever since I became old
all revived, ringing out in my ear.
A cherished voice calling me therein.

Small Blessing

Taciturn is morning sunlight today.
It looks at me, blinking.
I suppose calm morning sunlight also
has brotherly ties with evening sunlight anyway
but it does not shove my wrinkled skin.

As they say forest trees are healthful
I wash my face with tree breath.
Sunlight with a smile holds my hands.
My younger brother that died young unfairly,
I see him still smiling
in gentle and good hues.

Could the breath of that tree then be
my brother's living soul.
I clasp the tree trunk searchingly in my arms,
run my hand over the heart that has long suffered.
Saying we are closer than attached
my brother strokes me instead.
Morning binds us as one.

Justification in Patagonian Manner

It was fretfulness that made me go back.
Growing older and more fearful,
in a world growing smaller in hindsight
I was going to say when I meet the ninth heaven
that the visible cannot be all there is.
Myself more and more refractory, more and more fault-
    finding,
and high walls hedging me in, oppressing me,
though unable to hammer them down
I wanted to know what dragged me hither.

Feeling a vacuum all around, I even wanted to demand.
The Patagonian brow, spouting volcanic smoke,
disregarding me and vexed, is silent without reply,
and I though fearful and dreading could not turn back.
I wanted to ask if this is all, if this is the end here.

The seven-year-old lamb we roasted for food every even-
    ing,
the eyes of the lamb younger than my grandson derided
    me.
Thick streaks of rain falling from Patagonian sky,
where strings of ties all disperse like clouds,
I sever tenacious relations felt as noose.
In the rain you cannot even see your tears running down.

Blades of grass round me chafing the skin to injury,
they pierce my breast like knife blades.
A land where deaths nobody has gathered up
slowly rise up, long washed.
I don't know how many days on earth I have left

but I forget I swore not to come again;
in the hour nobody can be seen in the thick rain
the promised pardon strikes me painfully.

PART II

Moving

An antiquated book
I haven't opened awhile
falls into my arms, saying it's glad.
The paper still retaining body heat.

I thought I alone have grown old
but I see a book too waxes old.
Nothing familiar to me
forgets to show age.

I flick the dust and open the book,
dust I could not see flies about.
My shoulders on which the days I kept hidden,
with a will for a decorated living unawares,
now awaken and scatter dust.
(Yes, indifference was the hardest.)

Between meeting and parting
memory's string loosens,
and a chink in an unfilled time.
Wonder if the words I left behind
without hearing an answer
will fall fast asleep tonight after all.

Misty Hour

When I was a breathtakingly busy doctor
and at the crack of dawn sent away deaths collected over-
    night,
closing the two eyes, my voice low with self-reproach,
the mist outside the window showed bloody tears.
Or, did I wish to efface myself totally,
patients that gave up their bodies in resignation
became late spring's elder brothers to comfort me.

(When did the mist come near, I didn't even hear foot-
    steps but how has it soaked me all over; not knowing
    when it began, when it cleared, I just shivered with
    gathering chill.)

A message that a friend of about seven decades died
without contacting me, leaving a single memo.
Sighing sky and stillness darkly shutting,
distant mist comes near to wet my eyes.
Yet, hearing that in departure he looked peaceful at the
    back,
I will rest on the sole promise that he'd stay beside me.

Green is the wide field of a foreign land,
the brook murmuring calls me in reflection.
The dead are always quiet and tenderhearted.
Half-awake regrets like forenoon attachment
hide a penitent soul in the mist.

Shore of Souls in Repose

I chanced to hear a voice calling me pitifully
so I turned on my way, came to a sea I saw for the first
  time.
Roaming about the shore whose age is unknowable
battered youths drown in the sea;
before getting sicker, before wounds rankle,
I stroke my body worn out with floundering.

My past family members that speak pristine words,
I don't know how but you came and stroked me on the
  back
when I went through fire and water aghast
when one-tract sorrows turned me a blind man.
Could it be that the pity's power turned into a bruise.

Now there is nothing to expect or spare.
Mail has come, news departed,
curiosity given up and dispersed.
Years heaped up into a dead land for winds to rest in.
Life bruised terribly flutter in the vacant air.
Aged breaker, saying Pity, nuzzles the shore.

Surfclam or Potato Stew

Is it because I've lived far away too long,
marvelous and rare are friends leading the way
saying, What shall we eat when you return home,
it's as though heaven comes out of the door an instant
to shower ten thousand rays of sunshine.

Mother and father are gone far away,
my younger brother who shared bedding with me left al-
    ready.
Childhood buddies who swore to live together until death
one by one went away to somewhere, leaving clouds be-
    hind;
should I say I am lonely, or cold and feel empty,
I again stand beside my friend's grave in the rain.
Are you living all well and good together there.

The friend, who told me the potato in potato stew
is not plant but pig's spinal cord,
probably cannot compete with the palate of those friends,
who say handmade-noodles-with-surfclam is best for
    hangover
and down a glass of strong liquor, spoon up clear broth;
I found instant gimchi goes well with surfclam
but now in my old age just hold back tears
over a few glasses of strong liquor, which I cannot handle.

They tell me instant gimchi with surfclam, or boiling hot
    potato stew
isn't the right thing for me a doctor, but
you do not know. The unfair and red-hot
taste of countless false steps on a cliff edge,

the taste of wandering, seeking, desirous of hanging to-
    gether;
when could I, who search on for a zesty, deep, pungent
    place,
join others to live together.
Is that, I wonder, anyhow a thing of the next world.

Land Lying Idle

Taken in by a friend suggesting that he and I together get to own a small country house, as I'm a homeless vagabond, you never know how many times I opened colorful glass doors of real estate brokers' offices, rambling around whatever township of Gwangju of Gyunggi Province, wherever in Hongcheon of Gangwon Province, and hamlets unknown to me, so as to look at some land lying idle. My friend taking the lead, we looked at several plots, where a blend of nameless birds and all kinds of insects and weeds and wild flowers were idling together, eyeing one another. The land lying idle from first may do so in a different way, there was no singing or signs of moving.

As I leave a hamlet, feeling sorry about why the land lying idle doesn't show how they do that, I ask a countryman about the difference between the idle land and the occupied; he explains that the one is staying naturally as it pleases and the other so expensive that you dare not touch. That once houses are built, buildings erected, it gets hard to breathe, hard to see sunshine. I look back as I leave the village, *What, since when?* In sight is giddy heatwave and a round of dancing in natural colors. The land lying idle, I see, indeed rises to have a merry lark at last.

Ah, now I see. Why the land lying idle glared at us. Why it danced delightfully upon our takeoff. I see that it worried if it would live without seeing the sun. Sure, rollick, idle land, you must make merry swinging your body to make wild flowers, to dance joyfully, to call numberless insects. When you have much land lying idle, you breathe easy and sleep well. A flower, having washed her face, leans on a friend. You are so fair. The earth's laborious hand cradling the stinking and unsightly, then turning all into earth. Breaking into blossom, I loaf around airily.

Portrait of a Dancer

I look around, mother,
and see everybody doing well.
The stage and lightings and audience seats are doing well,
fervent human passion leaps alive
transported into a locus of wrestling inspiration.
Filling the stage is your arduous opinion
that the first original alone is art.

Your dreams dauntless though life was hard,
your steps majestic whatever the cost.
Saying that the end product of dance is human being, and
    wholly
burning away your life, creating dancing,
it is the conclusion of love received throughout life.
Mother, your warm

moves' ripple lives everywhere, the heart of your single-
    minded life is exquisite and strong. Pours into new-
    born rhythm the essence of life. One breaks free from
    the entire world's falsity. That courage is born dancing.
    Sets erect forsaken joy. Liberty living in dancing, pre-
    tense and embellishment hide underwater; unmasked
    liberty meets with liberty named otherwise.

Mother, your pride in headstrong persistence,
splendid are your soft fond moves.
Forsaken body and word at last come into bloom.

The Last/ Adjustment to Time Difference

After an all-day long flight I come at the earth's other side, stand before my house that's been waiting some two months quietly, gloomily. Lizards are busy noiseless, thousands of red bougainvillea flowers doze off in early summer sun. Daytime went by that way. Night came on, yet thirteen hours' time difference making no noise, I listened to Richard Strauss' "Four Last Songs." Listened in string to "Spring", "September", "When Falling Asleep", but no sleep, my entire body just got hot. Cries of the composer, who was singly moved by Zarathustra, grew raspy; a warm song of repose confessed only at the end. Anna Netrebko's voice envelops weary furniture even. The night I meet with Anna is deep and wide.

So I had to leave. However much I speak, you'd scorn that it's an excuse, time has since flown, I too have flown. A man in his eighties finds others' words and lives bright, novel, fascinating. I open a magazine I brought from Seoul. Past heavy poems and novels, there lies the last of the eighteenth-century Jean-Jacques Rousseau's writings, acknowledging his philosophical and literary failure. Call it *Reveries of a Solitary Walker*; He asks What am I, who have neither brother nor neighbor nor friend, I who have fallen away from all things. I go from the first walk to the tenth. How is the las conclusion going to fade away. Vague verbal expressions fade into the watcher's monologue.

After all, how many endings are there in the world, I wonder. Why does an ending carry weight. In 18th century one encountered during a walk his last piece of writing, in early 20th listened to a fervent last song. In gusty 21st century I only beg for a rusted sleep. In the scheme of things, adjusting to time difference could mean finding my place on earth. Is the changed address to which I, weary in body, head for, where I heard a mellow-stringed Korean harp in the house next to Woomyon Pavilion in Seochogu, if not, where I pursued the finesse of Kim Gyungah's flute music. In what meeting could I, all in a tangle, totally overcome time difference to be one true location. Which is to say, about when could we be of one body even beyond prejudice, hard to believe though.

If I, after pulling myself to go forward in several days, adjust to this day-and-night, bring up my devotion and supplication, could I overcome so much as years' of time difference? Rather long past, but could I see my late parents and be forgiven of my past irreverence. Even in my last days the world will ceaselessly flow on and I, unmoving, will be just watching the time difference lengthening. It's getting harder and harder for me to pursue to get hold of all souls sweeping by. The last time differences passing over there, the old age of superman is gone, none but cozy field's terrestrial heat comforts us to the end. Where has my body been? All lame pretexts, bondage. I see tough finale concludes only then, bright lives with no vertigo walk the same path with us.

City of My Younger Brother

Have you been well? I see you in bloom as late as early
    summer.
A hopeless afternoon, rain-sodden as soon as you bloom,
although I too left in aversion the city where we parted
is it telling not to come to visit often
or crooning in a familiar voice,
the rain soaking the ground to the strains of Taechoon
    Cheong's tune.
I tell you, I don't understand all of the repeated chant.

The epitaph obliterating the sweet solitary city,
some day we too will be obliterated
but stagnant water smells, rots and changes.
Let flow the days that were splendid, so they will shine and
    live.
In the region where wet land distantly trails away,
on the blurred border where sky begins
is the view of the moment we cannot part.

Morning rain stops only toward evening,
soft wind rises where rain clears.
Vibrant breaths wind-borne
has become gentle evening twilight today.
A city of red-yellow throws a dazzling festival.
Magnificent gloaming flaring out, forgive me,
I say I did not know how to love.

In the Shadow of Time

Fragile heart
contemplating spring flowers rapt,
hasten to grow old.
So that I could live through parting
heavier than rainclouds.

Spring rain moaning
and fog lingering
to my heart's hurt,
please soak no one.
So that meeting and parting
should fall into a long slumber.

The flower swept away in the rising wind,
where is it wandering, crying.
A path with no reply,
darkly diffusing
the fragrance of sleeplessness only.
Farewell, by all means.

Address of the Sunset

More than 50 years ago, in a foreign hospital emergency
    room
I think I let the bespectacled nice white old lady
die by my mistake somehow or other.
I cannot forget her utterly exhausted fair face.
In less than a week after coming to a remote alien land
I possibly misread the electrocardiogram, not my field,
and made error in my prescription, or in surgical operation;
while getting transferred to a sick room she died
and evidently I am to be blamed.
(I should have remembered her name at least)

For all that, dissembling and pretending to be a good doc-
    tor,
shameful body cloaked in white gown and smile,
in duty all through the night every three days
confirming with stethoscope the death I did not remem-
    ber,
writing up death certificate, surveying autopsy, over time
my expectant youth kept being thickly bloodstained.
My firm will with such confidence far gone,
how the dawn's gray space, when I stepped out of the hos-
    pital,
felt as though I was descending to a dark cellar.

Did I even breathe to live, those days of despair and la-
    ment,
in my little leisure I went up the deserted roof
and rent bit by bit, and some more, the gown I had on.
About how many gowns did I rend that year,
experiencing the burst of tears out of my belly.

Lack of money kept my home-coming just in my mouth
and then wandering in death-glaring insomnia
one evening I chanced to see on the roof
a far place behind the mountain, a silent sunset, that
    flower!

The sunset I saw in Seoul, flaring, promised me.
In that sunset were father and mother in the flesh.
Since that day I made up my mind to live again.
That warm and comfortable hue, in which I could see my
    country too,
I suppose it must still live somewhere.
About where in my home country could the sunset house
    address be.

Winter of the Artist Ed Hopper

One winter morning when I, past forties,
have taken up drawing, testing the water,
in the chill of New York, clad in a heavy overcoat
outmoded and out of fashion,
the shoulders heavy with depression and insomnia
are draped with iron bars of snow.
Old ages lie down on the sidewalk one by one
and the mute become pallid ice and live.

I step out of Ed Hopper's pub,
walk on with my coat collar hurriedly upturned,
but buildings with bowed heads simply shove me
and only the joints of my devoted days groan.
The city whose harsh winter's bone ashes
strike me on the cheek today again that I pay attention,
bruised air darkly swaddling the sidewalk
is turning into ice crackling.

Long ago I too was bursting with passion.
They say human bond is not limited to kinship only
and yet none has materialized into reality.
The artist still crossing a deserted alley,
the artist disappearing, eyes showing no possibility.

Taming Gossip 21

Beginning from my high school art class, 20th century French artist George Rouault's paintings were on my mind awhile then faded away, but I ran across him again while I lived crestfallen, extradited into a foreign country after college graduation and then military service. Rouault's original painting I chanced on in the gallery so cold with nobody inside gave me strength to live. Made me at long last lift my frightened, bowed head straight up. The painting I viewed was an etching of Jesus worn-out, head bowed, feeling forlorn. Ah, you the lofty one were also sad and lonely like me; I see you alone experienced and knew all the deep loneliness painfully engraved in my bones.

That sad face I met in my late twenties succored me as I lost my kin and wandered out in a foreign country; I perceive that the pillar I've leaned on in my life longer than five decades thereafter, without plan or scruple, was none other than you. And you spoke to me: World is cold and lonely and forlorn anyhow, but you must gather yourself up. I will hold your hand. So you even wiped tears on my blank face. The cross standing far away in the mysterious evening sunset hue, all things laid down. I too wanted to walk as quietly as George Rouault. Eventually I got a good grasp of that simple composition, mysterious colors, and the coarse *matière* completely healed my heart's deep wounds.

True, I realize that the world was a simple thing.
In the far backdrop a few diminutive men, a few
women.
The sun set, the darkness gathering,

now I also see clearly
where their footsteps are carrying them.
That your love alone is boundless,
a prayer in the growing dark
comes to me in contemplation.
You ask me where I am going in my quest?
That place is Hope.
The hope that I will see you,
an evening I go in quest of tired Jesus
standing, waiting for me again today.

Taming Gossip 22

In my old age, I tell you, a peculiar thing's getting smudged. My eyes are getting dirtied; bitten and ripped by occasional confusion, both my eyes are growing dimmer. The world not standing up to my scrutiny anyway, questioning whys and hows, I want to live as things stand but folks deride me, badger me, that I cannot see this or that. Oh well, who cares, I postponed and waited, then decided to have a cataract surgery. Had it on one eye, compared to the other, and find my vision so different. I might as well live the rest of my life fully, my body bright and fresh like my operated eye.

Growing old, my eyes don't function well, ears too are so weak that I often miss the point; no one tells me but I suppose my smelling's been weakened, appetite and even epidemic sensation have lost much of wholeness. Besides, the brain cannot be an exception, so, naturally I know that my cognitive quality or reasonable judgement gets muddled, and with errant memory I am becoming stubborn as a mule. Ah, that's why in old age we aren't able to feel the power that shakes our inner self, or the voice that calls us. Having been a doctor all my life, I cannot wholly trust so-called human cognizant capability or senses.

Who said what?
Really who said what?
The one who sees the invisible is human
the one who hears the inaudible is human
and rapture and salvation.
The one who can feel nothing
with cataract in the breast

with cataract in the heart
is a real grand blind man.
No doubt I perceive my vision, my hearing,
and all my senses at last
lock up, and prepare to depart.

Bird's Welfare

No, no, no.
Can't be my dead younger brother.
As I walk the trail that defeated the night
a bird crying at me,
flitting from branch to branch.
Calling plaintive, posing as if it knew,
no, no, no way.
It's been quite a while since he died....

Though I assure myself again and again
though I bend my neck, shake my head,
when the bird-cry abruptly ceases I hold
my chin up, look all sides for it,
no, no, it can't be my younger brother.
Empty sky in the direction the bird has taken,
that wind following the trail of
the sorrowful bird.

It's a Good Thing

My left leg has been throbbing in pain lately.
Seems to be aggravated as years go by.
Is it spinal cord compression, what-d'you-call-it, extruded
    disc?
doubtless degenerative change in old age.
How fortunate I got it after retirement.
How fortunate that it doesn't hurt when I'm asleep.
That I can walk without a limp....

In old age it's a routine to have a body part hurting
and a stroke of luck to make a man a shade humble.
Of course, it's a good thing that I couldn't be a rich man.
For I don't have to have eyes as cold as a frozen fish's.
To think slowly for want of energy
to talk rather softly and act slowly,
it's all good for my aging, easy-going brain.

The best are footsteps toward a place you likely heard of,
solace of the warm voice often heard on that path,
somebody says it all depends on how you think
but it's a good thing that I have a place ever to lean on.
When I wander and grope in the dark, when I am alone,
it's a godsend that I have a companion who holds my hand.

The Sinking Sea

Holding their breath, all fell asleep.
No regret even if not to wake up.
Words left behind shine
and the homeless lift up their heads.
Holding twin hands, fog became a star.

Standing before the sea these days
I can see but a fraction of it.
The rest, breakers with insubstantial noises,
seagulls also, heads buried under their wings,
neither cry nor move.
I see the breakers' rhythm, habitual and heedless,
has reluctantly been drenching all around
to utter the one word: Futile.

Neither can the shore quietly slip into sleep,
keeping vigil all night, shivering in cold.
Long ago I left without a word
the port of a sick age, where you had hard times;
the chill in my body, a mere compunction adrift.

Now is the moment to release the parting hand.
Words left on the face of waters
turn into wet salt;
familiar flowers
opening the sea gates then
thrusting out their young faces.

Late Autumn Cold

They say the culprit in cold is some virus
but weak immunity is greater reason,
so I'll have to catch the wind crossing over a mountain
and first ask tomorrow's destination.

No end to dizziness whirling in the back of my head,
fever and chill shaking my chest all over,
I see the sound of every flower fading and dropping to
    ground
was full-blown severe ringing in my ears.

How could there be a life with no story.
If asked of all the twists and turns, it may take everyone
    half a day;
having a difficult youth
wishing to grow old fast so as to walk a sure path
like a tiny flower seed taking off with eyes closed, oh me.

Tree branches that shed all the leaves overnight
had gooseflesh on their freezing twin arms.
Autumn yielded her shade to that bare tree
and showed me, who was waiting to be old with no one
    else,
the way colorful leaves and falling leaves take.
I no longer could leave the village.

The cold came to me like that.
Flowers that would lock up their doors toward evening,
now unable to shut the door even, head bowed feeble,
asked me *Shall we hold hands and sleep together?*

Were they, I wonder, simply asking for help.
Fallen for the word *we* I held *us* face to face
and exchanged persisting immunity and pathogens.
Fever from cold will perhaps abate in the teeth of keen
    wind;
I wished to pluck off with both hands the days to live on.

PART III

Flower of My Wife

Some trees
make large and most beautiful flowers;
some flower trees
take much interest in the petal color,
and one single flower is dazzling
when vibrant primary colors
or a thousand colors are harmonized into an embroidery;
some flower trees
are intent only on the fragrance to carry,
so the temptation giddily encountered in a flash
while walking round a street corner.

Now some flowers
with no reliable tree
with little size, color, fragrance,
apparently happy just to be alive
sway with a bland smile all the while.
When I see such flowers
I grow so comfortable, confident,
warm, relaxed,
that my shoulders feel featherlight, hence
I suspect they are yours,
and you greet me with your gentle flower hand
saying that the solitary journey was a face unadorned.

Morning Walk

When I walk in the long fog, trusting just my heedless eyes,
feeling like an exile with no more polluted crowd around
you, aged winds opening eyes stiffly
at the breath of gregarious oaks and Indian lilacs.

Last night, the breaths exhaled
where trees talked together in mutual distress
that they live with only bleak view in them. Soiled tough
    oxygen,
a shade blanched, is well mellowed.

Mellow oxygen, as I am still in the flesh
I drink you. My pulse wrinkled deep throbs.
This morning as we share living body heat
that wounded tree, that once told me a poem void of body
    heat is dead,
ever standing by my side.

Moving and breathing only is not living.
The older one grows, surprisingly the more charitable days,
tree's shade to rest in expands by armful each time.
Tree's fingers comfort the heart's core.

Monday's Shadow

On Monday
everybody takes a leave.
As flowers fade
all fade.

We faded away again.
Weekend was a battleground
and though the year turned
the failure did not alter.

In every void a shadow
is unfolding its own body.
You must go your way ever carefully, the slightest
error will rend the shadow.

While I wandered about the world
in search of the lost me
the shadow which was hidden inside the house
and raised me up with both hands,
I assure you to confess
the whole of my hidden past.

I am going to fully harvest all the hours
I abjured past few months, precisely
this summer long.
I will dry those grains well,
thrash and clean, then surely plant
with great care in this soil.

Young and Fresh Word

1

Young and fresh word is taken by the young,
deceitful word, racking its brain, simply reeks,
dismally aged word only rehearsing slow utterances
whirls round me, whose eyes are now dim.
Where to find newly budding word to hide ugliness of
old age.

Young words arise at daybreak every day
vigorously kicking off dew,
then breathing out hot breath only late afternoon
with an armload of living, thriving poems
heartily embrace their beloveds.
It seems there's nowhere I could squeeze myself in.

Now I'll have to gaze at the moon hard at midnight to
take down what the moon says, or secretly jot down
what the pumpkin flower says when blooming, or
at least the loud laughter of cabbage jerking its body
in the cabbage patch. If that doesn't go well, will it
do if I gather up what apples in a midsummer orchard jabber up, all their sayings, to dry them awhile
in the shade. If I cool and dry the heat or moisture
in their sayings, could I touch one word bright and
spicy as a pepper well-dried in the autumn sun. Fruit
or vegetable refrigerated and long frozen won't do,
as it'll crumble when dried. Words made by a racked
brain won't do either, for they from the outset will
feel flat uneasy. It is truly beyond the capacity of an
aged man to find a living word.

2

Places that I miss all ended up changing, really.
Gone is bright and hearty energy in the flower of my youth
which I cherished in my body,
my spirit too, then carefree, is now hazily dull.
Maybe darkened in the shade, even you I cannot see well.

Only now do I sense that my neighbor looks away.
Word like pain, word like regret,
wretchedly stuck like a fish hook in the throat,
the landscape at nightfall is yet awake clearer.
Or else, is it that I am having difficulty falling asleep.
The back, thus far imposing, is now stooped; the night
    lengthens.

Flight of the Elephant

Circa A.D. 200, when the elephants inhabiting the Yellow
    River basin
from before the Christian era fled to Yangtze River basin
for cold climate, the northern nomadic race also for cold
    climate
came to the southern district over time.
The slovenly, interminable migration vastly caused plague
and the survivors warily huddled together in herds.
Round the middle reaches of the Yellow River, the Sui and
    the Tang joined
but the population as many as nine million households
    dwindled to two million,
so too, the numbers of elephants decreased to less than
    half.
The remnant elephants crossed the border, fled to further
    south.

In 186 King Mongkut of the tropical country Thailand
    wrote a long letter
that he would give America precious elephants, a young
    healthy couple fled
from the north, as an expression of friendship.
A message with the advice to let him live in a very warm
    place:
Send us a ship for the elephant, and sufficient water and
    feed;
they may be used for hard labor or war, are also good for
    transportation.
The letter somehow came to America in no less than half
    a year;

President Abraham Lincoln distracted in the turmoil of
the Civil War
politely wrote a letter of rejection: As we have steam en-
gine
they are not needed for labor and war, and we cannot pas-
ture them for we have no jungle here.

Has it since been about a hundred years? A novelist named
Romain Gary
in middle Africa met the elephants in steady flight. Met
seared tears of the
elephants who got nervous at cruel gunshots, ears thus
growing bigger, and shot
to death by illegal poachers crazed for ivory, or starved to
death.
Just in Africa, 30 thousand of them each year were cap-
tured or died,
over last 50 years the elephants' blood must have made a
river.

The chased elephants are said to flee to gaping bogs in the
jungle,
loud is the wind that their time of extinction looms near
for foodstuff shortage, calves drowning in the bog, and
diseased to death.
The Guardian UK Daily in last April 19 edition,
quoting Dr. Smith's paper presented in the magazine *Science,*
said the first of mammals on earth destined to extinct is
the elephant.

Ancient Indians honored the elephant foremost
in appreciation of the shoulders shouldering the earth;
the elephant in the conception dream of Buddha's mother

or the one with Saint Bohyon of mercy and majesty on, or
the one that came eastward, Sutra on the back, are all
said to be past generation stuff we know of, like legend,
yet in my old age I clean forget grateful bonds, line by line.
If I have no strength to swim to Jordan or Nile Rivers
I must not be fooled by honeyed words, must at least
    guard my land.
The news that the elephant, head dropped, lately stopped
    fleeing,
the elephant stamping, the hidden heart drawn and lifted
    up!

Eye of the Great Oak

I thought this was a thoughtless tree
but now I see the living leaves all day long
are solely gazing at the hot sun.
Without a modicum of boredom or tiredness
regardless of all others' attention
his eyes, looking up to the brilliant sky.

That resilient concentration of ardor
could be the endurance against the heat;
not a drop of sweat,
with noonday's serenity and deep faith
he goes on, the tree's life in his arms.

I, whose thoughts are many,
am not capable of an instant's concentration,
even what I say out of firm conviction
I do not abide by a few days, a few months.
Increasingly restless probing
obstructs the front, darkens tomorrow.

A summer noonday, everyone gone,
tens of thousands of leaves in one direction
solemnly absorbed in stony silence,
the eye of the great obedient oak
that was my mentor all summer long.

Essence of Dew
—to the spirit of Kim Cheesu who departed earlier

The tolerant figure I saw when alive,
now dead, I see over my head.
Smile, voice, gait even
shining in the morning sun,
the essence of dew.

Dead or alive in good cheer,
so amazing and heartening is your passion
persisting in one solitary path
nearby or in the distance.

The body of dew wholly shining
widely smiling in the sun,
beauty transcends time.
Surmounts time's ragged wall.

Shadow of grass-blade well sodden
showing itself after dew fades away,
becoming soft water in the morning
to slake my thirst,
beloved dew of your face, now gone away.

Is the Lion Really a Poet, I Wonder

Is the lion really a poet? The lion prowling in the Serengeti Plain or the Savannah Plain, or in countries like Tanzania or Namibia, known to just sleep almost twenty of twenty-four hours a day. I'd think he'll have to dream often in sleep, what a lot of dreams has he in stock to be able to sleep so long. Is he the earthly king for the many and varied dreams, is it that in his great leonine head are stored nothing but dreams. How many dreams on earth has he kept, I wonder. I've heard a poet must abound in dreams, many a dream makes a good poet, could it be true?

Such a long time in sleep, and yet only average life span of twenty years as reported, his short life is akin to that of a prodigious poet, I should say. Apart from feeding time, he is known to awake only in the night, and gazes up at the countless stars flung in the skies. In such time, I think he recites a poem, muttering in their own language. When I was young I heard that a poet must have courage. Also, that in face of loneliness he must be majestic like a lion. I fled early because I was afraid of it. These days, however, it appears neither courage nor loneliness is a requirement for the poet.

That reminds me the lions at times haunted in Korea, too. The lions waking up in the dead of night and reciting poems in Mount Kuwol, Mount Jiri, or the valleys throughout the country: dreams of lions, that suffered losses for the many dreams and had a hard life, were wet with tears and reeked of sweat. They always longed for a cheerful country and wanted to live, writing poems. Now they have become our poetry, our land altogether, and yet,

I wonder where are the lost courage and dream living now. Don't they say only the poet of courage becomes a star when dead? In Korea's every nook and corner nameless poets who temper their roars, gazing up at those stars; lions.

Journal on the Trip to Ahndong

Early morning, assisted by a cab I went to Cheongnyangni
    Station
to meet the plant pathologist Dr. Lee Soongu,
rushed about at some entrances that have undergone great
    changes,
boarded the Central Line *Mugungwha* for Ahndong, passed
    Yangpyung.
Curious how far down autumn colors have reached
I am intent peering out; the outside waves, that it's glad to
    see me.
Through Wonju, Jaecheon, past Danyang, Punggi,
    Youngju,
peaceful Ahndong welcomes me, nestled between low
    mountains.
In front of the station I see the two, we for the first time
    greet mutually.
Like the village I lived in, perfect affection overflows.

I unpack in the spacious room in Gwangsan Kim's head
    house,
sit in the Takcheong Pavilion with Han Seokbong's grand
    hanging board,
and the appetite for Ahndong *soju*[1] isn't just an exaggera-
    tion.
Evening, walking the village to the trail with sweet old
    trees,
in the over-a-thousand-year-old Hall of Paradise in the
    Bongjeong Temple in Mount Cheondeung
one or two jumpy autumn leaves already drop off.

---

[1] Soju is Korea's strong liquor.

I can feel a thousand-year-old air on the twilight pillar.
The air, soft-hued and long-fermented, has sweet scent.
The doctor says he is happy to guide us
but the reason that smile looked like priceless jewel
is because it hid a grief for the loss of a good son.
I don't think I can touch that heart so vulnerable yet.

I slept myself out on the upper floor heated by firewood
then, slow walking, peered into right and left,
curious about how the village looks in the morning frosted
    clear and cool.
To Dr. Lee, I suppose, autumn will not come this year
    again.
To his paused life I wish to offer my shoulder.
I look far off, holding the soju bottle, daytime drink, un-
    finished.
I hear the laughter of his son whose face I haven't seen.
I think I know who ate Ahndong noodle in my place.
Perhaps it's not for anyone to take his turn
but after I depart from this world I wish to come to live
    in Ahndong.

Pray for Me!
—to my friend Gyuchang

I paid a visit to my old friend to ask how he's doing
since he had been abruptly paralyzed on one side from a
    stroke;
the bedridden friend
grabbing my clothe with his good hand
shouted out to me in an earnest voice.
Pray for me! Buddy, pray for me!

Good and precise and smarter than anyone,
reputed to be the best surgeon in the country,
just as intensely he said in tears.
Pray for me! Chonggi, please!
I don't think I am the only one asked,
but if you'll understand the prayer power of a shallow be-
    liever as me is weak
and the prayer offered in a loud voice so you could hear
    well
is going to be incoherent....
Really? Friend, sure, of course I will.

God, this friend who asks even me to pray,
please save him. Touch and comfort the intent
of this friend that seeks you at last, though late.
Before I knew it my prayer may have pervaded your body,
you smiled a slow, unexpected smile as though contented.
And I ended up shedding tears myself.

For my weak earnestness my friend improved very little,
and I returned home in half a year, visited him, found him
    cheerful;

he said he had peace of mind, thanked all
then within a little over three years left the world.
His wife's message: Word of gratitude was his last will; he
 closed
his eyes peacefully and thanked you, too, in acknowledge-
 ment.

True, all go this way, I think we will meet again.
Prayer, a conversation living and breathing.
A familiar voice in a flash comes at me.
Pray, please pray for me!
Who's that? That voice in me.

Anne the Red Hair

The heart of Seoul war-torn into a ruinous heap,
I was in middle school, always hungry,
when Anne the Red Hair emerged out of the blue.
To me that had never seen red locks
her face said to be full of freckles was a curiosity.
Envious of the Anne said to smile and cavort even when
    mistreated
I wanted to live ever savoring the joy of the young sky
but after the war dust only was whirling about the village
and what a pity that my dream lover should live in the
    West.

For a while days and months and years went by, and I aged,
yet a corner of my heart curious about Anne's wellbeing,
so to the northeast Canada in boat, in bus;
a hamlet called Charlottetown in Prince Edward Island,
how time, so long and rough, has bypassed the town,
trees with clustered red apples stand in row
along the rural roads tidy and quiet;
looking at the apples, looking at Anne's red locks,
and then seen on the dusty highway outside the town
a shabby wooden single-story building, standing apart,
    mismatched,
the sign 'Jaeju Restaurant' only is somehow registered in
    my memory.

Off the tourist bus, then the green-roofed Memorial Hall,
the old school and post office and downtown and hillside
    grove
are all arranged as they were in the old children's story;
maybe Anne's Memorial Hall, maybe the writer's grave,

the gravestone was wreathed in bouquets of fresh flowers.
These days whatever land I travel, I see Koreans living
    there
but my regret is that I didn't try out the dusty Jaeju Res-
    taurant
as I left the town known to have a constant traffic of tour-
    ists.

Sordid days of my childhood,
who would have known that I was to come to live here;
wanderlust, or rather shameful poverty driving me
from Jaeju Island all the way to the Canadian border;
had I taken a meal with spicy gimchi pot stew at Jaeju Res-
    taurant
and clasped the owner's hand, both speaking in Korean,
I guess I myself, before him, would have wanted a bottle
    of soju.
The Anne I loved turned hundred ten this year
but in the cheerful and animated Jaeju Restaurant
gimchi odor must have groped for and hugged the Red
    Hair, no,
could Ann have smiled, first having tofu pot stew?
Ann, over hundred now, will be my lover again
and home is a place one may go to, taking time in leisure
after this life comes to the end;
so far away therefore invisible but congenial,
that place, I think, would wait ever and ever.

So It Happened, But...

So it happened, but...
last night in the tangle of a dream awhile
I ran helter-skelter in the scanty clothing I had on
over the mountain, over the hill, through grassy field
like a runaway for self-preservation,
ran blindly, dashed breathlessly
to finally meet familiar people and yet,

This is Korea here?
(I don't remember running to the sea....)
A few people looked back
and with an air that said Is this old man crazy
voiced: Yeah, right. Never heard of another Korea.
Gladness swells up, yet in a dignified manner
holding back contented smile to myself
I bow in greeting, breaking into humming.
Not tired though I certainly have walked a whole lot,
I feel so happy that tears gather in my eyes.

Upon waking I think it over, so it happened, but!
With what strength I ran to such a distant place,
and exactly where in Korea it was,
I rack my brains but no way of knowing.
Such a distant country, and the idea of me just in under-
     clothes,
pushing through grass, running on all day!
Where was the place I reached, really.
It's already been several days since I had the dream
but my vivid curiosity has not died.

Bird Taking Leave

Good-bye now.
Don't get lost on your way
with your tender soul carefully in your arms,
don't forget your destination
and farewell.

Lost and wandering in the whirlwind,
confounded which way to take,
once I even shed tears.
In the midtown sky just filled with dust
I could not see future days with open eyes.
The feeble winging that oppressed my shoulders,
nobody called it soaring romanticism.
While I bore smarting pains the roads took leave
and the village I want to go to already shut the door.

Possibly for the delusion, living then dying,
or intoxicated by a shifty star in the thick of night,
I scoffed on end, not knowing for long
that those wild days I fluttered, searching back and forth
were actually the marks of a living life.

Supposing we meet again by whatever destiny
souls will then first have to say hello to each other
and watch if my breathing reaches you well
if your body heat comes to me with ease
past a long bridge.

Good-bye now.
However hard the journey,
I wish to God that you will in no way be hurt

that your pathway as you return
be ever bright and proper....

The South Sea at Night

God made the sea
and people opened the seaway.
The wooden boat shoulder-dancing nonstop
ran away with night sea that shook the stern,
the wind whimpering by the wooden ship
sleep talks awhile, then submerges.
The vow to share life to the end,
whence did it get lost to wander so.

Nightfall, the moon also undresses.
Still ashamed that they said they'd risk life
wet clothes are immersed in thoughts.
As they say that the body is indeed the mind's shadow
delicate moonlight that was in piercing agony
now enwraps the sagging shoulders;
the sea that had lone intention then hid himself
became midnight salt to light up all around.

Joyful Carol

Father passed away in autumn,
mother too in autumn later on. And
a precious friend of mine went on in autumn
and autumn is a place translucent and joyful,
it should be easy and joyful resting, mounting,
if acceptable I too would like to go in autumn.

What I heard: Somebody saying he's going to the heavens
gingerly escaped deep into colorful autumn leaves
and ended up hiding there
and another, fooled by sundry fruit scent,
hid himself in an orchard, knowing nothing about it.

In a weather like this, a song is a good analgesic
but why are the voids in the body hurting?
Is the reverse of hurting happiness, or misery.

Father was by himself that year too
and mother, to and from work
alighted on the tiring snowy road.
I too therefore grew light inside,
I can therefore still fly.
Is that sound your eternity or not.
The waterway I've hidden in me
flowing to no end, a blissfully empty day.

Self-Portrait 2

Viewing over twenty same size self-portraits
one by one in a row, beginning from Exhibit Room 1,
I was so sorry, strained and aghast that I sighed.
How destitute not having money to buy a model
and just keeping on painting self-portrait like this.
I wonder, was the artist Van Gogh not jaded.

Just how often have I labored with all my strength and
    sincerity,
giving my whole being to the world and literature.
Ashamed, in his Amsterdam art gallery
I reflect on how hard my life has been.
From somewhere a sharp cry of vainglory besetting me.

(Justification of the one who lived shivering with a damp
    fever:
Painted self-portrait out of desire to know self;
at thirty-seven without a lover or a neighbor
in the dark second floor room at the Auberge Ravoux, he
    died.)

Alive today, too! As in a newspaper article
empty weight of the one who has lived shallow and slick;
lost brutes who have lived without fortitude
out of calculation designed every year, every day;
conceivably my days on earth are numbered,
where should I go, and whom should I ask of my path.

The Angel's Lament

Nowhere to lean on, really. Parched moaning wherever I lie down, suffocated corpses wherever I go. A strange land with no place to rest a weary body was my wound. A raging pandemic smites the world, numberless dead bodies pile up and they say No place to bury or cremate them; the 60-year-old conceited oath that I would become a poet, belated but now I revoke it. Finding a place to breath comes first.

I cannot see you well. Gradually I grow fearful of the saying that when I leave this house I can see the glad country and we meet all, dance in tears. With what face should I greet you? It cannot be as luminous as sea stars, and yet the contradiction that I am in love with you even as I take a step back out of fear of suffering unprepared. The vow not to hate is on the run lest it be caught.

I thought I am a man without much greed, desirous of helping others. Thought all I had to do was suffer my fever. There were naked yet beautiful days, now what more to add and what more to conceal to be at ease. Before I knew it the age-ripped wind has ceased, and my soul hearkens to you. Only on hearing the seven difficult words, your ragged features by degrees grow clear.

Once I lived in harmony with wild flowers and winds, nevertheless where you were rejected bleeding was of dust and hollow earth and cairns; I too walked hungry the same path I believe you are still clambering the rocky mountain, with humanity's burdens on your back. Now may I tell you that I've been lonely for long? There was nobody in the ragged village to share my only play. Without even hearing me, they all walked away.

Bob Dylan, then a young man, mutters that in the wind is the answer. And asks how many times one must lift up one's head and search to see the real heavens. Yes, I too have lifted up my head innumerable times all through my life. Only in my old age I was awake to the fact that the great lies latent in the simple. The sun dips, time flows on in between you and me, and the heavens are but high and far as yet.

A medical student dissecting dead bodies all night, I simply rejected the food you offer. Because I believed I could live on my own. Only after those reeking times went by and I got ousted from my country, I understood that I am a hungry man. As I came round the alleyway to the world, and took your food in tears, only then was I barely able to keep my body and soul alive. O my refuge poor and unceasing.

Nature, liberty, detached sensibility streamed out of the right side of the brain meet with the dexterity of physical chemistry and blood seated in the left side of brain, and after an arbitrary discussion, shape me. What I learned while cutting that brain in pieces, ripping and poking another's heart, opening the visceral cavity: human being is a mystery made by somebody; at the end of the road an outstretched hand leading us home. A tinge of penance becomes my last will, and I bow low.

I often forget that a rainbow lives not in a bright and clean place but in a valley dark and stooped low. Dreams of varied size and shape were my aim. Inasmuch as the rainbow lives, I believed you too would return sometime. Who is the one standing over there stunned and consumed by pain. I hear a voice singing in *Stabat Mater*. There rises a magnificent rainbow, the pain overcome in the backdrop.

I see it is all but over. The one shuffling ahead, I am glad of the familiar figure from behind. I see that the sighs I've often heard in life were not to say I put no more expectations. The lament heard by the one fallen and bled, the signal to begin anew. I say I knew not how to open my eyes, hence neither the meaning of the sigh. That we all together rise up again, the angel's cherished lament in my ear!

There comes a day when every valley shall be filled in, every mountain and hill made low; the crooked roads shall become straight, the rough ways smooth.[2] Infinitesimal calculus, difficult as was, is all solved, the sunset going over the mountain has come to a halt. Now is the time for a sacrament for my life. I draw near to you who transform multiple sins and remorse into joy. A sea of souls in the evening glow; slowly rising upon wings, oh my shameful body.

---

[2] Luke 3:5

Rose, the Village Where John Lived

Finally it's disclosed that I am a sham.
A youth hanging only onto popularity lightly made up,
unstable earthly fireworks all at once setting off
to momentarily brighten my distressed shade
became winds' memory and then left.

In a country of science with too many right angles
likely for scent of money, or of perfume afloat,
within the formula that energy is the speed of a mass
a daily dreamer with a shabby look:
he liked John who spoke of an extraordinary world.

The next day the summer sun laughing like crazy
enclosed the impoverished village in which he lived.
Unclear whether past life, or next,
the most tenderhearted John, likely in dotage,
throws off all of the lowly and ignorant solitude.

The heart often aches.
What sickness, I wonder, killed the rose.
A penurious parting with no groaning left behind.
All rumors that stayed in the village faded away,
and a rare breathing by my side.
Who are you that chills my heart?
Though seemingly lonely as in youthful days
I could no longer live lightly.

Pain grows into heavenly glory.
Roaming about that small rocky mountain
I could recognize nothing
but your voice.

My kids I see two or three times a year,
knowing neither my poems nor my country,
pertly take as a half joke
when I say I'd better be buried in my homeland.

Raining, then clearing,
but remnant rains joined
to make a rainbow.
The John who says he wishes to be born once more
in this place where the rose is dying,
the angel's winging often heard
became your mouth, obliged to speak.
Love was ever so young
that it amazed us.

As We Must Meet Again

Please wait
as we must meet again.
Do not hide yourself or conceal
or change your countenance.
Though the intent cannot be different
will it be a youthful face when you smile for gladness,
or a crying face for a long suffering.

It is no fragrance just to be alive.
By ones and twos opening eyes in greeting,
buds spring out of the seed in the breast.
Flower seeds are so much light as to float on the water
and if a fairly good body, flies far.
The aches of a raw understanding
to lighten up more, even if forgotten.
The lowliest of attitudes, Hello?
where do they all join to live.

As we must meet again
a world I knew not opens itself.
The tomorrow full of beginnings,
which I desired to death.
I embrace my kin.
Let us not part again, the saying
rather wakes me up.

Commentary: Beyond Parting

Heejung Lee
(Poet, Literary Critic)

1. Expulsion, Immigration

This is a concise profile of Chonggi Mah, a poet and a
doctor residing in America. To make a long story short,
this says that he is a poet who lives in a country of envy,
holding a coveted job. A meticulous reading of his poems,
however, gives one a realization that such initial impres-
sion is remote from reality.

> I came to a foreign country on borrowed money.
> Worked day and night, paid back the loan,
> sold out remnant lonely springtime of my youth
> resenting the country to which I wouldn't be able to
>   return.
> The one-way road I've taken is but a solitary way lived
> without pretext or remorse or dismay or flattery,
> —From "Honor of Dew"

There were indeed unusual complications in his move
to America. The outset of misery was unforeseen, the process of redress long and exhausting. The world and those
who drove him to the unalterable "one-way road" "solitary way" became the targets of his resentment all along.
Whence came the peculiar place of exile, where pretext,
remorse, dismay, flattery cannot stand?

> in my youth I too lived in prison, gnashing my teeth.
> Dim air, gloomy walls, and fury hard to breathe,

82

may no country forcibly imprison and threaten and oppress
air or reed that live sinless.
Forbear overthrowing the other's unguarded life
by however big a name or idea or power.
Forbear confining, or striking
even if you suddenly find living hard and painful.
—From "Time in Prison"

Sharp edged words like illegal arrest, forced imprison-
ment, ideology, government power, torture, etc. denote
the 1965 events that shook up the young poet's life. It was
the military regime's retribution against the eminent literary men who signed against the Korea-Japan Conference.
The poet was then a soldier, and that caused further trou-
ble for him. It is not too long ago that readers got to read
in Mah's prose and poetry the particulars of this.

2. Poet, Doctor

Apart from the initial term, to wit, overseas immigration
stealthily enforced by the national authority, one cannot
understand the life and poetry of Chonggi Mah. With this
event as a turning point, his livelihood and dreams of literature, well on the way, unraveled, and the young man in
his late twenties was thrown into a strange land empty-
handed. The bright side of his continued "search for a way"
and "building a house" is that he was able to go on with
his pursuit as a doctor and a poet. His poetic march thus
continued, and readers in the homeland could continue to
read his poems.

Doctor and poet. Both are professions demanding extreme absorption. In general, a would-be professional
with excess talent seeks to concentrate by lowering the excess talent; a prodigious artist by neglecting his livelihood.

Chonggi Mah the poet coped with both. The experiences as a doctor fertilized his poetry, and his identity as a poet writing in the vernacular mitigated the solitude and nostalgia in an alien country.

> The medical science I had learned all I wanted was not
>   a learning
> but a hard stealing into human groaning,
> sinking into that darkness.
> A long road of sinking, then getting soaked.
> —From "A Night Walk in Sinseol-dong"

On that dark road by a stream in the homeland on his way to see some acquaintances, the poet looks back on his life. Medical science is a realm of cold science, but he does not confine himself to this mold; he rather took the business of peering into, and curing sick human body as an opportunity to heartily face humanity's sighs, joys and sorrows. While trying to understand by means of scientific principles the human body that lost the balance due to a disease, the act of comforting physical pain and mental discouragement as a healer, a helper, a comrade in life, could be rendered as "a hard stealing into human groaning" and "sinking into that darkness." Stealing and sinking into signify tearing down the division of two different areas for a fusion. This is to be one in sympathy, in as much as "sinking, then getting soaked"; hence no different from "to love all in earnest." The anecdote of recalling in the mien of an understanding patient a just-departed, cherished one, is a familiar recurrence in his enduring poems.

Mah gains a momentum to reflect his vocation and his situation through universal human sympathy shared with those who haunted the threshold of life and death.

Did I even breathe to live, those days of despair and
  lament,
in my little leisure I went up the deserted roof
and rent bit by bit, and some more, the gown I had on.
About how many gowns did I rend that year,
experiencing tears bursting out of my belly.
Lack of money kept my home-coming just in my
  mouth
and wandering in death-glaring insomnia,
and then one evening, I chanced to see on the roof
a far place behind the mountain, a silent sunset, that
  flower!

The sunset I saw in Seoul, flaring, promised me.
In that sunset were father and mother, living.
Since that day I made up my mind to live again.
That hue warm and comfortable, in which I could see
  my country too.
—From "Address of The Sunset"

This poem begins with his calling up from 50-year-old
memory a "bespectacled nice white old lady" whom he
met in an emergency room. She died during the transfer
from the emergency room to a sickroom, and the young
doctor was agonized wondering if he was to blame. Perhaps this is a hurdle fated for a man to stand between another's life and death. Self-reproach that he is an incom-
petent doctor drove him to despair as in "my expectant
youth kept being thickly bloodstained" in stanza two. The
above quote stands on the extension. Suffocation, despair,
lament in the extreme cause an unusual behavior as in
"rent bit by bit, and some more, the gown I had on." It
was an evening sunset in the western sky that imbued his
body, so much grieved as to feel "tears bursting out of my

85

belly," with strength "to live again." That sunset was no different from the one he saw in Seoul. The west was in the direction of his fatherland; it was when his parents were still living under the sky.

A poem unshapely and deplorable
I devotedly managed to finish exhausted.
With a trace of warmth still in my heart
I put my arms around it, prizing, caring.
On hearing that I love it, the poem
radiates brightness on the face. Ah,
a word and bodily warmth too is solace.
—From "Taming Gossip 20"

Conversing with a poem he composed, comforting each other— this is a scene not easy to encounter in his poems. He once confessed that in his life writing poems means, most of all, self-redemption and self-solace. This poem, though a recent work, offers a view of the record of his lifetime poems. A vessel carrying truthful records of the crux of experiences, while not shunning the rigor of responsibility, was poetry to him. His poetry writing was likely a lifeline holding him, as he staggered in the midst of a strange language, strangers, and strange environment. Poetry's place to him, a man who watches to discern and cure human life and death, was a space to record the highest tension and search; a haven in the heart's core to ponder on the memory of the place from which he was expelled.

3. Stream, River
This poetry book *The Angel's Lament* is the twelfth by Chonggi Mah who commemorates this year the 60th anniversary of his debut. Reckoned to have published roughly

one volume every five years, we will have to say that his poetry writing has been without hiatus, not to say prolific or unprolific. Readers come to see in this volume that the many-forked stream, which formed waterways in the topography of his poetry last 60 years, is still in flow, and that these streams converge into a wider river. The world of this poetry book, in terms of his poetic waterways, seems like a late autumn scenery. Among others, longing for the climate of the fatherland he left behind, for acquaintances back there; lingering regrets about late family members and siblings; self-awareness watching his fate as an exile; regrets of frustrated dream of returning home; burden and pride as one that cares for life; religious faith and love as a way of life; symbolism adopting as seeds such words as water, flower, bird, light, star, sunset, shadow; these wide or narrow waterways run just the same in this volume.

> Dew is honor of my flesh,
> comes early in darkness
> and leaves before morning comes into full bloom.
> Having lived abroad invisible,
> with the day breaking I take off my torn armor.
> Dead dew is a few drops of water,
> what a difficult and fearful resolution
> to love in all earnest.
> —From "Honor of Dew"

This poem sets the book in motion. Dew, one of Mah's fond substances, is the name of some water. This, along with flower, is a positive life image in Chonggi Mah's poetic world. Dew is a symbol of something precious that exists for an awfully short time and then vanishes; in this poem, the honor to the flesh as seen in the first line. To refer to the last line of the same poem, dew is a medal conferred to a prophet, as well as to his eye. Who can merit the honor, or medal, which is called dew? Considering that the lines 2, 3, 4, 5 form antitheses, the poet's life corresponds to the birth and death of dew. What can be the "torn armor"? I think the answer to these two questions is the flesh. On the other hand, who is the subject that praises the accomplishment of the flesh, after having lived a "tough life" ("Last Day of Winter") and now taking off tattered armor to reveal "a face unadorned"? It must be the soul. "To love in all earnest" is the deed done both by dew and torn armor; the commendation "what a difficult and fearful resolution" accounts for the soul's gratitude to and satisfaction with the flesh. Mah disclosed again in "Night Walk in Sinseol-dong" that his life is a journey of "loving in all sincerity." Here, as a way of life, love does not exclude religious meaning.

The poet Chonggi Mah had a tendency to not betray in so-called 'orthodoxy' literature his being a devout Catholic believer. Although he has written meditative poems to share with fellow believers, as compiled in *The Touch of the One Who Loves Me* (Daughters of St. Paul Press, 2007), with him as a coauthor, spherical distinction was strict. The manifestation of faith was limited to implied words like "blessed death" in his early vignettes. Blessed death is the abbreviation of "live good, die blessed", the Catholic Church phraseology used in place of "depart the world"; the import can be sufficient completion of religious rite as well. Mah used this term in a poem in memory of his late father. In the first place, his faith originates from his father; the self-reproach that early on, after much suffering, his abrupt departure from parents may have caused the latter's sudden illness, and the remorse that he was unable to be with the latter at his death, are thought to have strengthened Mah's faith.

Belief in God deemed to be the pillar of his life, to wit, the world of love, forgiveness, promise, is the main current of this poetry book. The title poem "The Angel's Lament" is a weighty work composed recently. The opening presents an attitude of reflecting on his own life hitherto as a doctor and a believer, observing the world.

> Nowhere to lean on, really. Parched moaning wherever I lie down, suffocated corpses wherever I go. A strange land with no place to rest a weary body was my wound. A raging pandemic smites the world, numberless dead bodies pile up and they say No place to bury or cremate them; the 60-year-old conceited oath that I would become a poet, belated but now I revoke it. Finding a place to breath comes first.

> I cannot see you well. Gradually I grow fearful of the saying that when I leave this house I can see the glad country and we meet all, dance in tears. With what face should I greet you? It cannot be as luminous as sea stars, and yet the contradiction that I am in love with you even as I take a step back out of fear of suffering unprepared.
> —From "The Angel's Lament"

The first stanza depicts the disastrous outbreak of the Corona virus. This happened in the land where Mah, a poet, a doctor, and a believer, had lived half a century. He revokes his earlier oath to become a poet. Deploring his own state of affairs after giving up the noble promise with you, now merely seeking "a place to breathe", the poem goes on to the next stanza. He cannot see God nor himself.

And so, even the dream to enter into the "glad country" has turned a fearful thing. Preoccupied with avoiding suffering from this world, he is not confident to long for that bright world. The next six stanzas, followed by the above-quoted, reiterate sotto voce his life as a doctor and a believer. In this process of reflection and remorse, he comes to an understanding that the naked, the estranged, the hungry, and the suffering are identified with himself, and further, with God he believes on.

> I see it is all but over. The one shuffling ahead, I am glad of the familiar figure from behind. I see that the sighs I've often heard in life were not to say I put no more expectations. The lament heard by the one fallen and bled, the signal to begin anew. I say I knew not how to open my eyes, hence neither the meaning of the sigh. That we all together rise up again, the angel's cherished lament in my ear!

> There comes a day when every valley shall be filled in, every mountain and hill made low; the crooked roads shall become straight, the rough ways smooth.[3] Infinitesimal calculus, difficult as was, is all solved, the sunset going over the mountain has come to a halt. Now is the time for a sacrament for my life. I draw near to you who transform multiple sins and remorse into joy. A sea of souls in the evening glow; slowly rising upon wings, oh my shameful body.
> —From "The Angel's Lament"

These are the last two stanzas. The key word of the first of these is the sigh, that is, the lament. It is a sound

---

[3] Luke 3:5

Mah has "often heard in life." Contextually, the lament "heard by the one fallen and bled" should be understood not so much as of themselves but as of somebody invisible who is watching them. Somebody that heaves a deep sigh in the face of the tragedy, Mah believes, is an angel. He is awake at last to the fact that the lament signifies "Begin anew!", brings to realization that "we all together rise up again." The last stanza ushers in the time God comes to the world again. Now God's roads are prepared smooth, the poet has finished "infinitesimal calculus, difficult as was", which is an orderly lifetime assignment. His time has come to a pause. The poet drawing near to God who transforms multiple sins and remorse into joy, his body is full of shame.

4. Existence, Faith
A man is standing before Mighty Nature.

It was fretfulness that made me go back.
Growing older and more fearful,
in a world growing smaller in hindsight
I was going to say when I meet the ninth heaven
that the visible cannot be all there is.
Myself more and more refractory, more and more
    fault-finding,
and high walls hedging me in, oppressing me,
though unable to hammer them down
I wanted to know what dragged me hither.

Feeling a vacuum all around, I even wanted to demand.
The Patagonian brow, spouting volcanic smoke,
disregarding me and vexed, is silent without reply,
and I though fearful and dreading could not turn back.
I wanted to ask if this is all, if this is the end here.

The seven-year-old lamb we roasted for food every
    evening,
the eyes of the lamb younger than my grandson derided
    me.
Thick streaks of rain falling from Patagonian sky,
where strings of ties all disperse like clouds,
I sever tenacious relations felt as noose.
In the rain you cannot even see your tears running
    down.

Blades of grass round me chafing the skin to injury,
they pierce my breast like knife blades.
A land where deaths nobody has gathered up
slowly rise up, long washed.
I don't know how many days on earth I have left
but I forget I swore not to come again;
in the hour nobody can be seen in the thick rain
the promised pardon strikes me painfully.
—"Justification in Patagonian Manner"

The man facing Mighty Nature is Mah himself, the
place Patagonia, the northern end of the continent where
he has lived a little over half a century. It's where the South
Pole ice and the volcanic fire meet, where the greatest two
of world's seas bifurcate. He feels fear. Active volcano
shoots up smoke, blades of grass sharp and spiky as knife
block the way.

He came here again, dragging his weary body. He who
says has grown in his old age more fearful, more refractory,
more fault-finding, has come a long way fretfully, for he
had something to say, something to ask about. Something
to say is reassurance of the fact that "the visible cannot be
all there is"; something to ask, "Who dragged me hither."

He is one that saw nothingness of the visible, one that wonders about his own destiny.

Mighty Nature gives no reply. "Spouting smoke" as if angered, she pays no attention to the poet's question. The sentence that he wanted to be assured of before Mighty Nature he now alters to "Is this all here", an interrogative sentence. Still no answer. To his downcast eyes, the little lamb served on the dining table seems to deride him. This is possibly an expression of a sense of shame, with his own unreasonable act objectified; but I think what he saw in the dead lamb's eyes was absurdity and grief of ephemeral things. The lamb is not the subject of derision, but in itself an illustration of fate of the finite.

In the last scene the poet, frustrated by Mighty Nature's silence without reply, gazes up at the sky "where strings of ties all disperse like cloud", at the rain streak that "severs all tenacious relations felt as noose." "Strings of ties" and "tenacious relations" are all human affairs, finite beings' affairs. And he sees that this is a land where "deaths nobody has gathered up / slowly rise up, long washed." Inorganic Mighty Nature does not kindly tend to finitude of the finite. This detachment lies not just in the difference of time scope of that history.

He has been to this place before. About ten years ago, here, he wrote a poem entitled "Lamb of Patagonia." In it he, looking at "some skies" afloat above "a wild field", recollected somebody's advice: "Didn't I tell you, even if I do not feel love / please just believe that I exist somewhere?" Unassured yet of love's presence, he rather focused on the story of the poor lamb dying by brutal fate in barren land, and wound up the poem with "The lambs I met on South American border kept on dying / so I could not begin my story I have still kept buried." Rhetorically, in this poem he told all he had to tell. Because the lamb's fate was a representation of the fate of all finite beings, including humans. On the one hand, if he rightly kept his story buried, as goes his wording, we can consider that in this "Justification in Patagonian Manner" he has begun his own story untold in "Lamb of Patagonia."

He did not find flower in the borderland called Patagonia. I read in "Justification in Patagonian Manner" the heartscape of the poet, who stands at the borderline of religious realm and existential realm. In this poem one doesn't see flower and love, more often than not centerpieces in in Chonggi Mah's poems, but "love" runs through the heart of that "Lamb of Patagonia." In his poems "love" holds both existential and religious import. In the "Lamb of Patagonia" he did not achieve his purpose of confirming love's presence, but ultimately shifts the center to religious realm in "Justification in Patagonian Manner" by concluding "the promised pardon strikes painfully." Just as the Himalayas is gods' abode to those living in Nepal, the Patagonia was God's abode to Mah who's been living in America.

5. House, Origin
It is said that Mah spent his infancy and boyhood in Tokyo, Japan, his birthplace, and also in Masan, Gyeongnam, his mother's home, and so on; but we can say the one in Myeongnyun-dong, Seoul, where he spent his adolescence until leaving the fatherland, is his home. There's a poem in which he set down his intimate feelings visiting the "old home I used to live in as a child" in Myeongnyun-dong. It is "Earth from Seoul", and it carries his 50-years-later follow-up visit to the house, now another's residence, scooping in the yard "a handful of earth" into a pocket before

leaving. The earth, being "a handful of my old family's fond voices and laughter", feels "soothing and heart-warming."

Should I happen to go suddenly in an alien land
please ensure to put this handful of earth in my hand.
—From "Earth from Seoul"

This he said to his wife. The alien land is America, and "go" a synonym of departure from the world. He attempted a few times at permanent homecoming, but without success. After an early retirement in 2002, he wanted to spend longer times in the fatherland, but that went amiss. As time passed the new family in the alien land naturally planted its roots deep therein. To the children, now grown up and having a new family of their own, father's alien land became their homeland, and father's homeland their alien land. Meanwhile the old family in the homeland immigrated to the alien land. Permanent homecoming now has become a permanent hope to him. The testimony in another poem "Rose, the Village Where John Lived", as goes "My kids I see two or three times a year / pertly take as a half joke / when I say I'd better be buried in my homeland", informs that he and his children are under strictly different practical circumstances. Considering a statement like "Not all people can die in the countries of their birth" ("Gallipoli 2"), he seems to have accepted living the rest of his life in the alien land as reality. His hope takes a step back to the point of saying "after I depart from this world I wish to come to live in Ahndong" ("Journal on the Trip to Ahndong"). Let us now return to the story of earth.

Won't it be too meagre to hold in my hand when I
    leave.
Sometimes it even shines with luster as if saying some-
    thing.
I suppose the hardest thing of all is parting
but when I peer into my earth even parting is tender.
On the road I pass by I see someone too, who left my
    side.
—From "Earth from Seoul"

A handful of earth he takes to America, and treasures
it. And draws solace from touching and peering into it,
against worry and sorrow for parting shortly to come. The
last quoted line pictures his heart made ready to serenely
accept the event of leaving this world. "Someone who left
my side" are those who predeceased him. Now their
epiphany is common to him. Experiences of seeing the
departed, or feeling their presence was not rare in his past
poems; most of them were his kindred. A house is the
foundation of life; a family or a family member is a living
community, or a destiny-sharing group, partaking in that
foundation. With the flow of time, a house becomes antiquated, family members grow up or old. One remembers
the house that was a shelter against darkness and foul
weather, together with the mountains and rivers made familiar while growing up. One leaves the house of his own
origin, and old family, to establish his own house and family; this is repeated through generations. Mah, after a long
time, visited the old home of his origin, came to "old family's fond voices." With a good many of them no more in
this same world, their voices are the more precious. There
are also several poems in this book written in memory of
the departed family members.

I look around, mother,
and see everybody doing well.
The stage and lightings and audience seats are doing
      well,
fervent human passion leaps alive
transported into a locus of wrestling inspiration.
Filling the stage is your arduous opinion
that the first original alone is art.
—From "Portrait of a Dancer"

Watching a dance performance, he misses his mother who was a dancer. The above quote is the first stanza, in which he reports that even after her departure the art she dearly loved is just as before. Stage, lighting, audience seats are doing well, and particularly, "fervent human passion" and "wrestling inspiration" just the same, then comes his reminiscence of her view: "The first original alone is art." This poem is wholly dedicated to his mother. There are some poems depicting his longing for a younger brother.

My younger brother that died young unfairly,
I see him still smiling
in gentle and good hues.

Could the breath of that tree then be
my brother's living soul.
I clasp the tree trunk searchingly in my arms,
run my hand over the heart that has long suffered.
Saying we are closer than attached
my brother strokes me instead.
Morning binds us as one.
—From "Small Blessing"

On a forest path lit by morning sun, he sees his younger brother in smile. The latter, who was attached to the former all his life, came to quit newspaper reporter job over a political matter, traversed the sea to live near his brother, and then died in an accident. He is still close to the poet's heart, to come to life in pity and sorrow at a quiet time. A walker is holding a tree long. His heart has long ached over his younger brother's affairs, and today the younger one came near as a tree to comfort the sorrowing brother. Another day, the younger brother appears in the form of a bird also ("Bird's Welfare").

6. Parting, Meeting
The spirit of parting pervades this poetry book. The poet does not forget all along that he has reached the "twilight age" with "a body that has tumbled down" ("Leave-taking of the Seas"), an old man "bent with age" ("Stranger's House"). A time of parting often becomes an object of supposition and imagination.

> 1: "I have no remorse even if this night walking mark my end."
> —From "Night Walking in Sinseol-dong"
> 2: "completely old and wizened, / then drop off into twilight shadows,"
> —From "Vespers"
> 3: "Father passed away in autumn / [.....] / if acceptable I too would like to go in autumn."
> —From "Joyful Carol"
> 4: "I don't know how many days I have left on earth"
> —From "Justification in Patagonian Manner"
> 5: "Conceivably my days on earth are numbered"
> —From "Self-Portrait 2"

There's no need to exaggerate illustration 1. By the context of "Night Walk in Sinseol-dong", the reason for his imagining an "end" could be his feeling at ease while staying in his native country. "Drop off" in illustration 2 is a further extension of figurative speech, comparing life to flower. "Vespers" is a poem extolling the happiness of the one who "merely has a single flower." The single flower is a presumable manifestation of his intrinsic religious faith and life goal; yet, to focus on the envoy of the poem above, it also appears a metaphor of physical life, in short, life. Illustration 3 is the forepart of "Joyful Carol", one fine autumn day's reflection on life and human relations to this day. The day of departure is pictured in bright and joyful language. Illustration 4 is from the end part of "Justification in Patagonian Manner" as reviewed above; illustration 5 from the closure of "Self-Portrait 2" in which he, viewing Gogh's self-portraits, is lead to search his own life. These two illustrations carry "days on earth." Which is coupled with "days in heaven." The indication of such leaving or "parting" in this book does not automatically complete itself.

Mother and father are gone far away,
my younger brother who shared bedding with me left
    already.
Childhood buddies who swore to live together until
    death
one by one went away to somewhere, leaving clouds
    behind;
should I say I am lonely, or cold and feel empty,
I again stand beside my friend's grave in the rain.
Are you living all well and good together there.
—From "Surfclam or Potato Stew"

Parents are gone far away, and younger brother and childhood buddies went away to somewhere. With the passage of time, those who shared love and friendship one by one leave, and he imagines that perhaps this "somewhere" is one and the same place. Not quoted here, this poem's envoy "when could I join others to live together / Is that, I wonder, anyhow a thing of next world" betrays a hope of being with them where they are. He calls that place "the next world." To those who believe reincarnation that could be another life, but in his world view it is a postmortem world. Another poem "Misty Hour" contains this statement upon hearing that his friend died: "Still, hearing that in departure he seemed peaceful from behind / I will rest on the sole promise that he'd stay beside me." To him, people upon death don't disappear altogether. Upon promise "they can stay beside me" even after death. This here, a world of both the body and materials, is not far from that there, a world of the mind and soul. "Promise" often appears in salient parts of Chonggi Mah's poems. Promise is a human effort to take control of even a fraction of indefinite future time. We take advantage of this to arrange and share actions for the not yet time. This can occur between man and man, between God and man.

One can imagine or promise "meeting" after "parting." Here, meeting means a world beyond parting. In "True, all go this way, I think we will meet again" ("Pray for Me") and "Gradually I grow fearful of the saying that… we meet all, dance in tears" (The Angel's Lament"), the readers have a glimpse of the 'beyond parting' imagined by the poet. A poem brightly and happily showing meeting after parting, "As We Must Meet Again", appears at the close of the book.

Please wait
as we must meet again.
Do not hide yourself or conceal
or change your countenance.
Though the intent cannot be different
will it be a youthful face when you smile for gladness,
or a crying face for a long suffering.

It is no fragrance just to be alive.
By ones and twos opening eyes in greeting,
buds spring out of the seed in the breast.
Flower seeds are so much light as to float on the water
and if a fairly good body, flies far.
The aches of a raw understanding
to lighten up more, even if forgotten.
The lowliest of attitudes, Hello?
where do they all join to live.

As we must meet again
a world I knew not opens itself.
The tomorrow full of beginnings,
which I desired to death.
I embrace my kin.
Let us not part again, the saying
rather wakes me up.
—"As We Must Meet Again"

In this monologue-based poem, the first four lines and
the envoy in stanza two, with their endearing speech, look
great. Those addressed to in a sweet manner are the departed. "Please wait" is uttered by the one just taking off.
The restless poet pictures the gestures and countenances
he will face again in the next world. "Do not hide yourself
or conceal / or change your countenance" means: Let us

101

meet bare body, bare face. And then he weighs whether gladness will come first, or deep emotion, i.e., pathos, and simply enjoys it per se, seemingly not very concerned for distinction. The "intent cannot be different" is the truthful meaning of meeting again, with great joy and deep emotion united in one. "Fragrance" in stanza two, I think, is something that sustains individual essence though disembodied; I read it the heart, that is, the soul's identity.

The seeds in the hearts of the glad begins the itinerary of life as designed. Plant seeds by nature takes off to a new and different world by means of water, wind, animal skin or belly. Remembering the matrix, they reproduce it somewhere else. Flower seeds, in their lowliest position in new soil, sprout to raise stalks and make flower buds. May we read "lighten up, even if forgotten" like flower seeds, as a sort of teaching, as the poet's realization that it'll be good and right to understand sufferings as a process of discipline? It's then natural that this realization is "raw" and "aching." It seems his life was indeed pushed away like seeds flying far off, yet accomplished a paradoxical assignment to lighten up amid sufferings and sorrows, even if forgotten. The conclusion of stanza two is a speech by the one that just arrived.

At the head of stanza three, he arrives at a village called "the tomorrow full of beginnings", led by "a world I knew not." This is the place "which I desired to death." In this village Mah embraces his "flesh and blood." They are at once his kinsfolk and representatives of all he has parted from throughout his life. As revealed in the last line, the reason why all of the account turns out a "dream" is probably because the poet is still on this side of the world.

7. Poet, Experiences

I see in *The Angel's Lament* a great forest of pathos, contemplation and remembrance cultured by an outstanding lyrical intellect, with his eighty-or-so years' experiences. The poet Chonggi Mah's linguistic tool, which gained full scope and refinement early on, has recently achieved with the passage of time stability and maturity; with added distinctive experiences in his body and mind handling the tool, his poetic world has grown vast and luxuriant. The readers will find happiness walking the luxuriant forest flung wide before their eyes, tracing in their reading the fine grains of continuation and transition.

Afterword

Poetry is a way of expressing love; a book is a sharing and an expedient for surviving the discipline in life. At least I believed it so, and have lived my life in love with poetry. If poetry's aim is not love, I do not need such. It is because the world is cruel, lonely, and difficult than it appears. Poetry must be an instrument of healing wounds in the bleak world. It may be because I was a medical doctor by profession. My concern always was with life and death, with pain and sacrifice and care. All the rest to me were mere gestures, husks, and untrustworthy things.

When I was a doctor it was cardinal to see closely and precisely what I saw, crucial to hear plainly and distinctively what I heard. The reason why I write poems anyhow is because I want to see invisible things, and hear inaudible things. Should a poet not attempt at seeing invisible things, what good would his so-called sensibility or imagination do anywhere?

Chonggi Mah

About the Author

Chonggi Mah, the poet, was born in Tokyo, Japan, in 1939. He graduated from Yonsei University, College of Medicine, in Seoul, Korea, and subsequently attended graduate school at Seoul National University. Shortly after coming to America in 1966 he was certified with the American Board of Radiology. He then worked as a professor in the Radiology Department of the Medical College of Ohio, and later as a pediatric radiologist at the Toledo Children's Hospital until his retirement in 2002.

Earlier in 1959 he made his debut as a poet through Hyundae Munhak, thereafter published *Quiet Triumph* (1960), *Second Winter* (1965). *Well-Tempered Clavier* (Anthology; Vol. 1, 1968; Vol. 2, 1972), *Borderland Flower* (1976), *Invisible Land of Love* (1980), *Are Reeds the Only Ones That Live Together* (1986), *Color of That Country* (1991), *Eye of Dew* (1997), *You Can Smell Tree in Birds' Dream* (2002), *Are We Calling Each Other* (2006), *Flesh of The Sky* (2002010), and *Forty Two Greens* (2015). His other publications include *The Collected Poems of Chonggi Mah* (1999), selected poems in *For It Is No Hope to Wish for the Visible* (2004); collections of prose: *The Joy That Has Not Yet Ended* (2003), *I Lived Calling You* (2010), *How Much We Together* (2013), *Beloved, Much the Same As Our Distance* (2014).

He has received the Korean Literary Award, the Pyonwoon Literature Award, the Yeesan Literature Award, the East West Literature Award, the Hyundae-Munhak Award, the Dujin Park Award, the Daesan Literature Award, The Academy of Arts of the Republic of Korea Award, and the Yonsei Man of the Year Award (2018).

About the Translator

Youngshil Cho holds a Master of English & English Literature from Chonnam University, Korea. A recipient of numerous grants for her English translation of modern Korean literature, she has translated and published eight contemporary Korean poetry books including *Bukchon* by Shin Dalja (Homa & Sekey Books, 2023), and *Forty Two Greens* by Chonggi Mah (Codhill Press, 2020).

She has authored three books, and *Everlasting Ring* is her most recent collection of poems. "If I Become Good at Math, Could I Solve the Skies", "Frozen Pond" and other poems written by her for young adults have appeared in some quarterly literary magazines of Korea.

www.ingramcontent.com/pod-product-compliance
Lightning Source LLC
Chambersburg PA
CBHW032105080426
42733CB00006B/427